CHUNG-GUN
and
TOI-GYE

CHUNG-GUN and TOI-GYE
OF TAE KWON DO HYUNG

By JHOON RHEE

Chung-Gun and Toi-Gye are two of the hyungs required
by the International Tae Kwon Do Federation.

OHARA ⓟ PUBLICATIONS, INCORPORATED
BURBANK, CALIFORNIA

I would like to express my sincere appreciation to my photographers,
Mr. Jimmy Rudd
And
Mr. Ku Kyung Chung

Thirteenth Printing 1984

ISBN 0-89750-003-2

PREFACE

Although introduced only recently in the western world, the art of Tae Kwon Do has become increasingly popular in all countries and with all age groups. Originally conceived in Korea as a measure of unarmed self-defense, Tae Kwon Do has blossomed into an art that is now practiced all over the world.

This book has been written with several purposes in mind. First of all, it is intended to develop a greater appreciation and understanding of Tae Kwon Do, which would contribute toward the growth of this ancient martial art. Since it includes explicit instructions and detailed guidance on all aspects of the art, it will serve as a basic text for beginners. To the intermediate students, this text provides a firm foundation for the more complicated patterns and advanced techniques which follow. It also serves as an authoritative reference on all phases of Tae Kwon Do training for the instructors.

CHUNG-GUN and TOI-GYE is the fourth in a series of five volumes covering nine of the major hyungs of Tae Kwon Do. The first book deals with the Chon-Ji hyung required at the white belt level. The second book deals with Tan-Gun and To-San which are required at the gold belt level. The third book deals with Won-Hyo and Yul-Kok which are required at the green belt level. The two hyungs in this book, Chung-Gun and Toi-Gye, are required at the green belt level. The other book in the series will deal with Hwa-Rang and Chung-Mu which are required in order to obtain the black belt.

It is my most sincere wish that this book will embody the true essence of Tae Kwon Do — the discipline and humility which arise from one's dedication to the art. Without such spirit, the student's training is incomplete; with it, he becomes master of himself. For both the physical and spiritual fulfillment of Tae Kwon Do, then, this book is humbly dedicated.

Jhoon Rhee

SENATOR MILTON R. YOUNG
President — U.S. Tae Kwon Do Association

AUTHOR JHOON RHEE

CONTENTS

WHAT IS TAE KWON DO?

Tae Kwon Do is a Korean martial art which has been developed through centuries of Eastern civilization. Today Tae Kwon Do has evolved into not only the most effective method of weaponless self-defense but an intricate art, an exciting sport and a trenchant method of maintaining physical fitness.

Many think that breaking boards and bricks is what Tae Kwon Do consists of, but this is an entirely mistaken concept. Demonstrations displaying such feats merely show the power and speed the human body is capable of utilizing through Tae Kwon Do training.

Tremendous skill and control are required in Tae Kwon Do. While blocking, kicking and punching techniques all contribute to making Tae Kwon Do one of the most exciting and competitive sports, its challenge lies in the adept use of techniques without having any actual body contact. Complete control over punching and kicking movements is paramount in stopping just centimeters short of the opponent.

Through the coordination of control, balance and technique in the performance of hyungs (patterns), Tae Kwon Do is regarded as a beautiful and highly skilled martial art. It is also one of the most all-around methods of physical fitness since it utilizes every single muscle of the body and is considered the ultimate in unarmed self-defense. In Korea, the Presidential Protective Forces are all trained in Tae Kwon Do and several other countries are adopting it into the training programs of their protective forces as well.

WHAT ARE HYUNGS?

One of the more important aspects of Tae Kwon Do training is learning Tae Kwon Do hyungs, a set series of attacking and defensive movements which follow a logical, predetermined sequence. Although each hyung comprises different movements or techniques, there are certain basic elements common to all:

1) Each hyung begins and ends from the same point.
2) All movements are performed at speeds and rhythms conforming to those established by the hyungs being performed.
3) All movements must be performed with rapid facing and correct posture.

Each hyung in itself is of immense value in the physical and mental development of the student since it serves many purposes. As a means of physical conditioning, it develops the student's balance, muscle coordination and endurance which ultimately leads to increased self-discipline.

Hyungs also give the student the opportunity to practice the ideal blocking and attacking movements against an imaginary opponent. Just as the student in school learns to print, so his handwriting is a departure from the ideal and becomes a mark of his personal style. The same may be said for Tae Kwon Do. A student's sparring or fighting style becomes his adaptation of the principles he has acquired from hyungs. The hyungs, then, are the student's line between Tae Kwon Do training and actual fighting.

Finally, hyungs are a graphic demonstration of the art of Tae Kwon Do that is a mark of the level of development the student has acquired. As a student progresses he undertakes more complex hyungs. They are designed to challenge and make him call upon his resources and all that he has learned in order to perform the new movements and increase his scope of discipline and development.

Tae Kwon Do hyungs have been developed and perfected throughout the centuries by the outstanding teachers of the art. Each hyung consists of the most logical movements of blocking, punching, striking or kicking possible within that sequence of movements. A student should not attempt to take on a new hyung until he has perfected the hyungs he is required to learn at his level of achievement. Before advancing to another hyung it is customary for a student to perform the one he is presently learning at least 300 times.

WITH WHAT HYUNG
DOES EACH RANK TRAIN?

HYUNG	RANK (Class)	COLOR BELT	AMOUNT PERFORMED
Chon-Ji	10th & 9th	White	At Least 300 Times
Tan-Gun	8th	Gold	At Least 300 Times
To-San	7th	Gold	At Least 300 Times
Won-Hyo	6th	Green	At Least 300 Times
Yul-Kok	5th	Green	At Least 300 Times
Chung-Gun	4th	Blue	At Least 300 Times
Toi-Gye	3rd	Blue	At Least 300 Times
Hwa-Rang	2nd	Brown	At Least 300 Times
Chung-Mu	1st	Brown	At Least 300 Times

REQUIREMENTS FOR 1ST DEGREE BLACK BELT

1. Right attitude and good character.

2. Mastery of the aforementioned nine patterns.

3. Capability of breaking three, one-inch pine boards with the following techniques:

   a. straight punch

   b. knife-hand strike

   c. front or roundhouse kick

   d. side snap kick

4. Good free-sparring ability coupled with well-controlled techniques.

5. Ability and willingness to teach the tenets of Tae Kwon Do to others.

CHUNG-GUN HYUNG

Chung-Gun is named after the patriot An Chung-Gun. The 32 movements in this pattern represent the age at which Mr. An was martyred in prison in 1910.

DIAGRAM

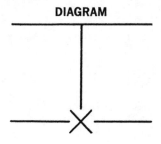

CHUNG-GUN
AT A GLANCE

READY   1

7   8

14   15   16   17   18

24   25   26   27   28

SIDE VIEW

BACK VIEW

OTHER VIEW

STEP DIAGRAM

CHUNBI SOGI
(Ready Stance)

Assume a closed ready stance "B" with left open hand covering right fist at solar-plexus level.

NOTE: All pivotal turns indicated in degrees, either clockwise or counterclockwise, refer to the directional turn of the face. Star symbols (*) indicate KIHAP (yelling).

FRONT VIEW

TOP VIEW

APPLICATION

BEGINNING FRONT VIEW

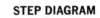
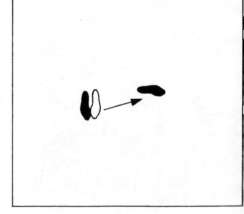

INTERMEDIATE FRONT VIEW

OTHER VIEW

STEP DIAGRAM

1. CHUNGDAN YOK SUDO
(Middle Reverse Knife-Hand)

Step out to the left with the left foot, assuming a right back stance as you execute a middle block with the left reverse knife-hand. ✶

FINAL FRONT VIEW

TOP VIEW

APPLICATION

21

STEP DIAGRAM

 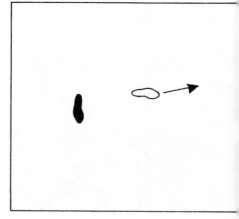

FINAL FRONT VIEW

2. HARDAN
AP CHAGI
(Low Front Snap Kick)

Execute a low front snap kick with the left foot without changing hand positions.

TOP VIEW

APPLICATION

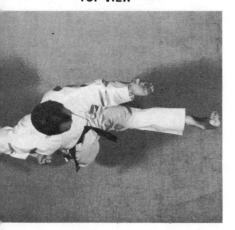

23

BEGINNING FRONT VIEW   **INTERMEDIATE FRONT VIEW**

OTHER VIEW   **STEP DIAGRAM**

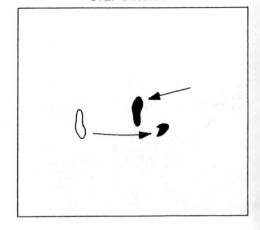

FINAL FRONT VIEW

3. CHANGKWON OLYO MARKI

(Palm Heel Upward Block)

Step down with the kicking foot, then step forward with the right foot, assuming a left rear-foot stance as you execute an upward block with the right palm-fist.

TOP VIEW	APPLICATION

BEGINNING FRONT VIEW

INTERMEDIATE FRONT VIEW

OTHER VIEW

STEP DIAGRAM

FINAL FRONT VIEW

4. CHUNGDAN YOK SUDO
(Middle Reverse Knife-Hand)

Pivot on the left foot 180 degrees clockwise, assuming a left back stance as you execute a middle block with the right reverse knife-hand.

TOP VIEW

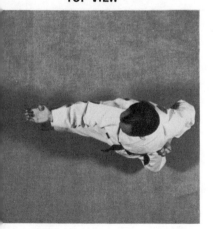

APPLICATION

OTHER VIEW

STEP DIAGRAM

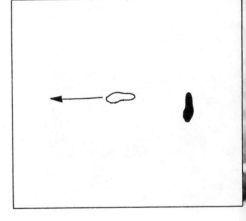

5. HARDAN AP CHAGI
(Low Front Snap Kick)

Execute a low front snap kick with the right foot without changing hand positions.

FINAL FRONT VIEW

TOP VIEW

APPLICATION

29

BEGINNING FRONT VIEW

INTERMEDIATE FRONT VIEW

OTHER VIEW

STEP DIAGRAM

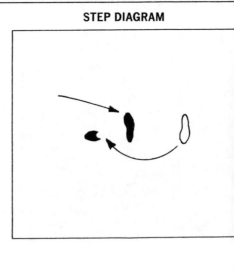

FINAL FRONT VIEW

6. CHANGKWON OLYO MARKI

(Palm Heel Upward Block)

Step down with the kicking foot, then step forward with the left foot, assuming a right rear-foot stance as you execute an upward block with the left palm-fist.

TOP VIEW

APPLICATION

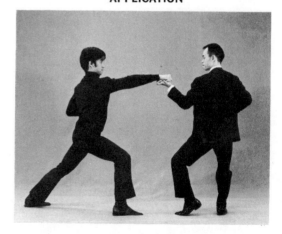

BEGINNING FRONT VIEW

INTERMEDIATE FRONT VIEW

OTHER VIEW

STEP DIAGRAM

FINAL FRONT VIEW

7. CHUNGDAN SUDO MARKI
(Middle Knife-Hand Block)

Pivot on the right foot 90 degrees counterclockwise, assuming a right back stance as you execute a middle guarding block with the left knife-hand.

TOP VIEW   **APPLICATION**

BEGINNING FRONT VIEW

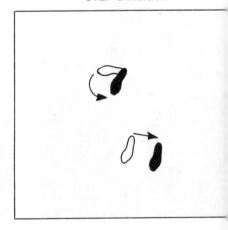

INTERMEDIATE FRONT VIEW

OTHER VIEW

STEP DIAGRAM

34

FINAL FRONT VIEW

8. SANGDAN PALKUMCHI TAERIGI
(High Elbow Strike)

Slide the left foot forward, assuming a left front stance as you execute a high elbow strike with the right elbow.

TOP VIEW

APPLICATION

BEGINNING FRONT VIEW

INTERMEDIATE FRONT VIEW

OTHER VIEW

STEP DIAGRAM

9. CHUNGDAN SUDO MARKI
(Middle Knife-Hand Block)

Take a straight step with the right foot, assuming a left back stance as you execute a middle guarding block with the right knife-hand.

FINAL FRONT VIEW

TOP VIEW

APPLICATION

BEGINNING FRONT VIEW

INTERMEDIATE FRONT VIEW

OTHER VIEW

STEP DIAGRAM

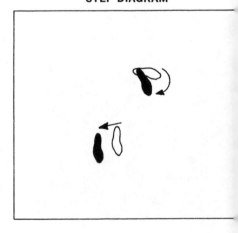

10. SANGDAN PALKUMCHI TAERIGI
(High Elbow Strike)

Slide the right foot forward, assuming a right front stance as you execute a high elbow strike with the left elbow.

FINAL FRONT VIEW

TOP VIEW

APPLICATION

BEGINNING FRONT VIEW

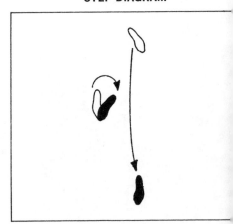

INTERMEDIATE FRONT VIEW

OTHER VIEW

STEP DIAGRAM

11. SANGKWON SEWO CHIRUGI
(Twin Vertical Punch)

Take a straight step with the left foot, assuming a left front stance as you execute a high twin punch with both vertical fists.

FINAL FRONT VIEW

TOP VIEW

APPLICATION

BEGINNING FRONT VIEW

INTERMEDIATE FRONT VIEW

OTHER VIEW

STEP DIAGRAM

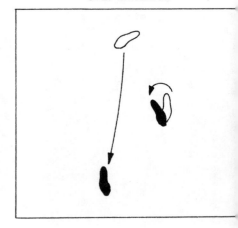

FINAL FRONT VIEW

12. CHUNGDAN TWICHIBO CHIRUGI

(Middle Overturn Punch)

Take a straight step with the right foot, assuming a right front stance as you execute a middle overturn punch with both fists.✶

TOP VIEW

APPLICATION

BEGINNING FRONT VIEW

INTERMEDIATE FRONT VIEW

OTHER VIEW

STEP DIAGRAM

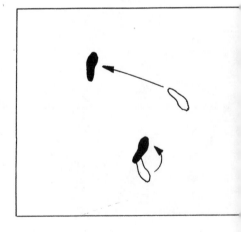

13. KYOCHA JOOMOK CHUKYO MARKI
(X Fist Rising Block)

Move the left foot about two shoulder-widths to the left and pivot on the right foot 180 degrees counterclockwise, assuming a left front stance as you execute an X fist rising block.

FINAL FRONT VIEW

TOP VIEW

APPLICATION

BEGINNING FRONT VIEW

INTERMEDIATE FRONT VIEW

OTHER VIEW

STEP DIAGRAM

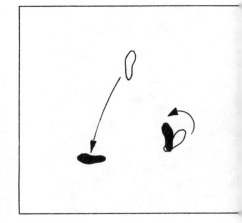

14. SANGDAN YIKWON TAERIGI

(High Back-Fist Strike)

Pivot on the right foot 90 degrees counterclockwise, assuming a right back stance as you execute a high back-fist strike with the left back-fist.

FINAL FRONT VIEW

TOP VIEW

APPLICATION

BEGINNING FRONT VIEW

INTERMEDIATE FRONT VIEW

OTHER VIEW

STEP DIAGRAM

15. JOOMOK BAEGI

(Removing Grabbed Fist)

Slide the left foot forward and assume a left front stance as you pull the left forearm inward, twisting it until the left palm faces upward.

FINAL FRONT VIEW

TOP VIEW

APPLICATION

49

SIDE VIEW

STEP DIAGRAM

FINAL FRONT VIEW

16 SANGDAN PANDAE CHIRUGI
(High Reverse Punch)

Execute a high reverse punch with the right fist.

TOP VIEW

APPLICATION

BEGINNING FRONT VIEW

INTERMEDIATE FRONT VIEW

OTHER VIEW

STEP DIAGRAM

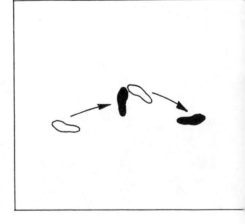

FINAL FRONT VIEW

17. SANGDAN YIKWON TAERIGI
(Middle Back-Fist Strike)

Bring the left foot alongside the right foot, then step to the right with the right foot, assuming a left back stance as you execute a high back-fist strike with the right back-fist.

TOP VIEW

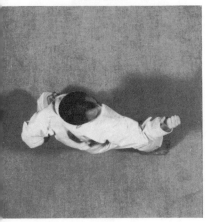

APPLICATION

BEGINNING FRONT VIEW　　　　**INTERMEDIATE FRONT VIEW**

OTHER VIEW　　　　**STEP DIAGRAM**

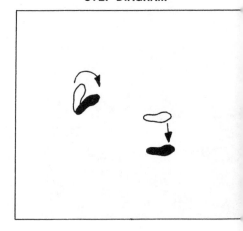

18. JOOMOK BAEGI

(Removing Grabbed Fist)

Slide the right foot forward and assume a right front stance as you pull the right forearm inward, twisting it until the right palm faces upward.

FINAL FRONT VIEW

TOP VIEW

APPLICATION

55

OTHER VIEW

STEP DIAGRAM

19. SANGDAN PANDAE CHIRUGI
(High Reverse Punch)

Execute a high reverse punch with the left fist.

FINAL FRONT VIEW

TOP VIEW

APPLICATION

57

BEGINNING FRONT VIEW   **INTERMEDIATE FRONT VIEW**

OTHER VIEW   **STEP DIAGRAM**

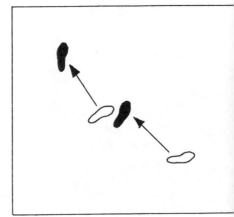

FINAL FRONT VIEW

20. SANGDAN DO PALMOK MARKI
(High Double Forearm Block)

Bring the right foot alongside the left foot, then take a straight step with the left foot, assuming a left front stance as you execute a high double forearm block with the left forearm.

TOP VIEW

APPLICATION

BEGINNING FRONT VIEW

INTERMEDIATE FRONT VIEW

OTHER VIEW

STEP DIAGRAM

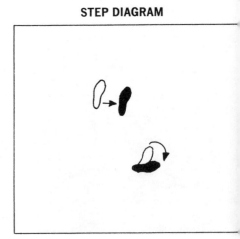

21. CHUNGDAN YOP CHIRUGI
(Middle Side Punch)

Pull the left foot inward, assuming a right back stance as you execute a middle side punch with the left fist.

FINAL FRONT VIEW

TOP VIEW

APPLICATION

BEGINNING FRONT VIEW

INTERMEDIATE FRONT VIEW

OTHER VIEW

STEP DIAGRAM

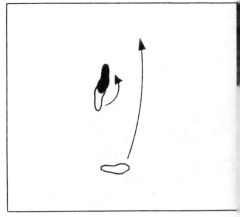

FINAL FRONT VIEW

22. CHUNGDAN YOP CHAGI
(Middle Side Thrust Kick)

Pivot on the left foot as you execute a middle side thrust kick with the right foot.

TOP VIEW	APPLICATION

BEGINNING FRONT VIEW

INTERMEDIATE FRONT VIEW

OTHER VIEW

STEP DIAGRAM

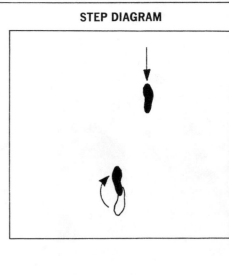

23. SANGDAN DO PALMOK MARKI

(High Double Forearm Block)

Take a straight step with the kicking foot, assuming a right front stance as you execute a high double forearm block with the right forearm.

FINAL FRONT VIEW

TOP VIEW

APPLICATION

BEGINNING FRONT VIEW

INTERMEDIATE FRONT VIEW

OTHER VIEW

STEP DIAGRAM

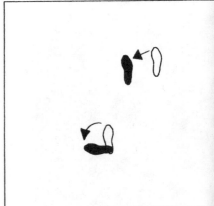

24. CHUNGDAN YOP CHIRUGI

(Middle Side Punch)

Pull the right foot inward, assuming a left back stance as you execute a middle side punch with the right fist.

FINAL FRONT VIEW

TOP VIEW

APPLICATION

BEGINNING FRONT VIEW

INTERMEDIATE FRONT VIEW

OTHER VIEW

STEP DIAGRAM

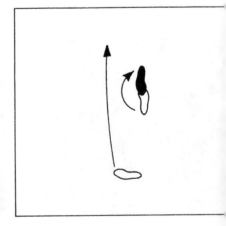

25. CHUNGDAN YOP CHAGI
(Middle Side Thrust Kick)

Pivot on the right foot as you execute a middle side thrust kick with the left foot.

FINAL FRONT VIEW

TOP VIEW

APPLICATION

BEGINNING FRONT VIEW

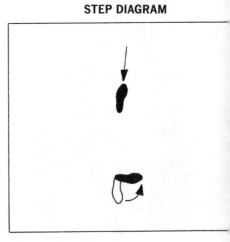

INTERMEDIATE FRONT VIEW

OTHER VIEW

STEP DIAGRAM

FINAL FRONT VIEW

26. CHUNGDAN PALMOK DAEBI MARKI

(Middle Forearm Guarding Block)

Take a straight step with the kicking foot, assuming a right back stance as you execute a middle forearm guarding block.

TOP VIEW

APPLICATION

BEGINNING FRONT VIEW

INTERMEDIATE FRONT VIEW

OTHER VIEW

STEP DIAGRAM

27. CHANGKWON NOOLO MARKI
(Palm-Fist Pressing Block)

Slide the left foot forward, assuming a low left front stance as you execute a pressing block with the right palm fist.

FINAL FRONT VIEW

TOP VIEW

APPLICATION

BEGINNING FRONT VIEW

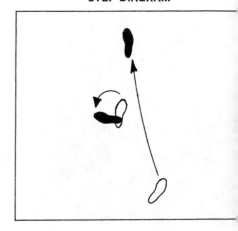

INTERMEDIATE FRONT VIEW

OTHER VIEW

STEP DIAGRAM

28. CHUNGDAN PALMOK DAEBI MARKI
(Middle Forearm Guarding Block)

Take a straight step with the right foot, assuming a left back stance as you execute a middle forearm guarding block.

FINAL FRONT VIEW

TOP VIEW

APPLICATION

BEGINNING FRONT VIEW   **INTERMEDIATE FRONT VIEW**

OTHER VIEW   **STEP DIAGRAM**

29. CHANGKWON NOOLO MARKI

(Palm-Fist Pressing Block)

Slide the right foot forward, assuming a low right front stance as you execute a pressing block with the left palm-fist.

FINAL FRONT VIEW

TOP VIEW	APPLICATION

77

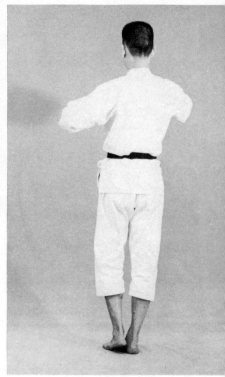

BEGINNING FRONT VIEW   **INTERMEDIATE FRONT VIEW**

OTHER VIEW   **STEP DIAGRAM**

78

30. BARRO DAEBI SOGI
(Upright Guarding Stance)

Bring the left foot alongside the right foot as you pivot on both feet 90 degrees counterclockwise, assuming a closed stance. Bring the right fist in front of the left chest horizontally.

FINAL FRONT VIEW

TOP VIEW

APPLICATION

BEGINNING FRONT VIEW

INTERMEDIATE FRONT VIEW

OTHER VIEW

STEP DIAGRAM

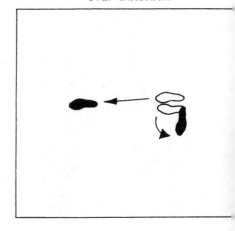

31. MONGDOONGEE MARKI

(Stick Block)

Take a straight step with the right foot, assuming a right fixed stance as you execute a stick block.

FINAL FRONT VIEW

TOP VIEW	APPLICATION

BEGINNING FRONT VIEW

INTERMEDIATE FRONT VIEW

OTHER VIEW

STEP DIAGRAM

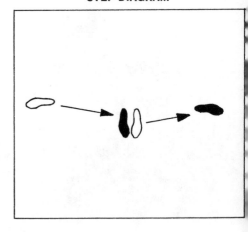

32. MONGDOONGEE MARKI

(Stick Block)

Bring the right foot alongside the left foot, then step to the left with the left foot, assuming a left fixed stance as you execute a stick block.*

FINAL FRONT VIEW

TOP VIEW

APPLICATION

SIDE VIEW

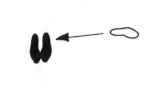

BACK VIEW

OTHER VIEW

STEP DIAGRAM

FRONT VIEW

GOMAN
(End)

Bring the left foot alongside the right foot, assuming a closed ready stance "B" with left open hand covering right fist at solar-plexus level.

TOP VIEW

APPLICATION

TOI-GYE HYUNG

Toi-Gye is the pen name of the noted scholar Yi Hwang, an authority on neo-Confucianism. The 37 movements of the pattern refer to his birthplace on the 37th degree latitude, and the diagram represents the word "scholar".

DIAGRAM

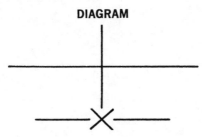

TOI-GYE AT A GLANCE

READY   1   2   3   4

10   11   12   13   14

20   21   22   23   24

29   30   31   32   33

5   6   7   8   9

15   16   17   18   19

25   26   27   28   28A

34   35   36   37   END

SIDE VIEW

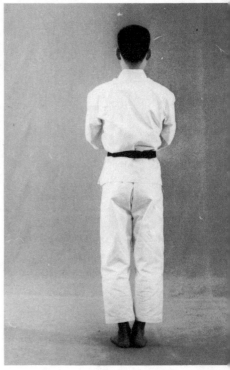

BACK VIEW

OTHER VIEW

STEP DIAGRAM

FRONT VIEW

CHUNBI SOGI
(Ready Stance)

Assume a closed ready stance "B" with left open hand covering right fist at solar-plexus level.

NOTE: All pivotal turns indicated in degrees, either clockwise or counterclockwise, refer to the directional turn of the face. Star symbols (*) indicate KIHAP (yelling).

TOP VIEW   **APPLICATION**

BEGINNING FRONT VIEW

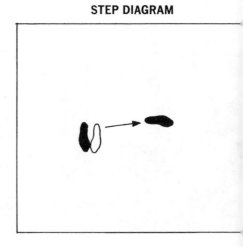

INTERMEDIATE FRONT VIEW

OTHER VIEW

STEP DIAGRAM

1. CHUNGDAN YOP MARKI

(Middle Side Block)

Pivot on the right foot 90 degrees counterclockwise, assuming a right back stance as you execute a middle side block with the left inner wrist. ✴

FINAL FRONT VIEW

TOP VIEW

APPLICATION

BEGINNING FRONT VIEW

INTERMEDIATE FRONT VIEW

OTHER VIEW

STEP DIAGRAM

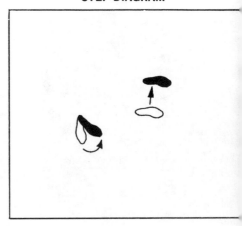

2. HARDAN KWANSU
(Low Spear-Finger)

Slide the left foot forward, assuming a left front stance as you execute a low spear-finger thrust with the right hand.

FINAL FRONT VIEW

TOP VIEW

APPLICATION

BEGINNING FRONT VIEW

INTERMEDIATE FRONT VIEW

OTHER VIEW

STEP DIAGRAM

FINAL FRONT VIEW

3. SANG-HARDAN MOASOSO MARKI

(High-Low Closed Stance Block)

Bring the left foot alongside the right foot, assuming a closed stance as you execute a high-low block with both forearms.

TOP VIEW	APPLICATION

BEGINNING FRONT VIEW

INTERMEDIATE FRONT VIEW

OTHER VIEW

STEP DIAGRAM

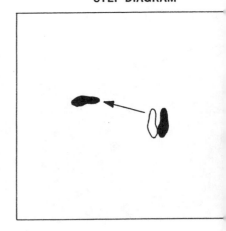

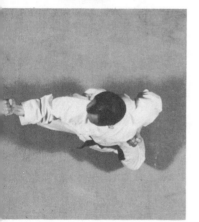

FINAL FRONT VIEW

4. CHUNGDAN YOP MARKI
(Middle Side Block)

Pivot on the left foot 90 degrees clockwise, assuming a left back stance as you execute a middle side block with the right inner wrist.

TOP VIEW

APPLICATION

BEGINNING FRONT VIEW

INTERMEDIATE FRONT VIEW

OTHER VIEW

STEP DIAGRAM

5. HARDAN KWANSU

(Low Spear-Finger)

Slide the right foot forward, assuming a right front stance as you execute a low spear-finger thrust with the left hand.

FINAL FRONT VIEW

TOP VIEW

APPLICATION

BEGINNING FRONT VIEW

INTERMEDIATE FRONT VIEW

OTHER VIEW

STEP DIAGRAM

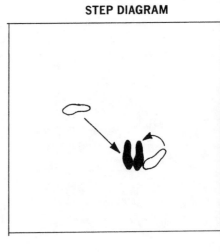

FINAL FRONT VIEW

6. SANG-HARDAN MOASOSO MARKI
(High-Low Closed Stance Block)

Bring the right foot alongside the left foot, assuming a closed stance as you execute a high-low block with both forearms.

TOP VIEW

APPLICATION

BEGINNING FRONT VIEW   **INTERMEDIATE FRONT VIEW**

OTHER VIEW   **STEP DIAGRAM**

7. KYOCHA JOOMOK NAERYO MARKI

(X Fist Down Block)

Take a straight step with the left foot, assuming a left front stance as you execute a low X fist down block.

FINAL FRONT VIEW

TOP VIEW	APPLICATION

BEGINNING FRONT VIEW

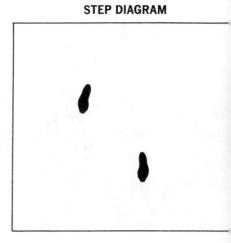

INTERMEDIATE FRONT VIEW

OTHER VIEW

STEP DIAGRAM

8. SANG KWON SEWO CHIRUGI
(Twin Vertical Fist)

Execute a high punch with a twin vertical fist.

FINAL FRONT VIEW

TOP VIEW

APPLICATION

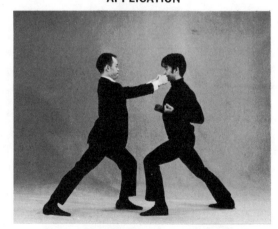

OTHER VIEW

STEP DIAGRAM

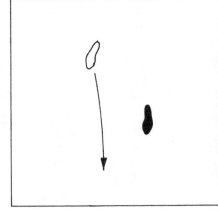

FINAL FRONT VIEW

9.CHUNGDAN AP CHAGI
(Middle Front Snap Kick)

Execute a middle front snap kick with the right foot without changing hand positions.

TOP VIEW

APPLICATION

BEGINNING FRONT VIEW

INTERMEDIATE FRONT VIEW

OTHER VIEW

STEP DIAGRAM

FINAL FRONT VIEW

10. CHUNGDAN CHIRUGI

(Middle Punch)

Take a straight step with the kicking foot, assuming a right front stance as you execute a middle punch with the right fist.

TOP VIEW

APPLICATION

BEGINNING FRONT VIEW

INTERMEDIATE FRONT VIEW

OTHER VIEW

STEP DIAGRAM

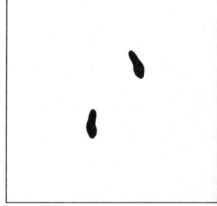

FINAL FRONT VIEW

11.CHUNGDAN PANDAE CHIRUGI
(Middle Reverse Punch)

Execute a middle reverse punch with the left fist.

TOP VIEW

APPLICATION

113

BEGINNING FRONT VIEW

INTERMEDIATE FRONT VIEW

OTHER VIEW

STEP DIAGRAM

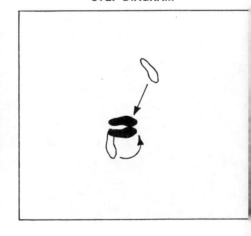

FINAL FRONT VIEW

12. MOA SOGI
(Closed Stance)

Bring the left foot alongside the right foot while you pivot on the right foot 90 degrees counterclockwise, assuming a closed stance as you pull both fists to their respective hips.

TOP VIEW

APPLICATION

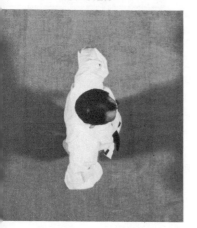

BEGINNING FRONT VIEW

INTERMEDIATE FRONT VIEW

OTHER VIEW

STEP DIAGRAM

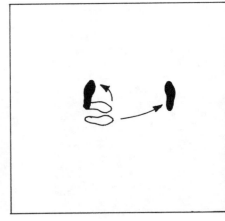

13. SAN MARKI

(Stamping W Block)

Pivot on the left foot 90 degrees counter-clockwise, assuming a riding stance by stamping down with the right foot as you execute a W block with both forearms.

FINAL FRONT VIEW

TOP VIEW

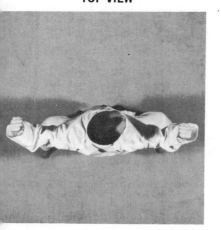

APPLICATION

BEGINNING FRONT VIEW

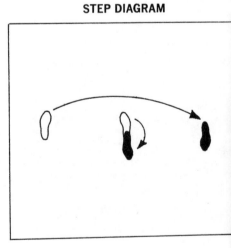

INTERMEDIATE FRONT VIEW

OTHER VIEW

STEP DIAGRAM

14. SAN MARKI
(Stamping W Block)

Pivot on the right foot 180 degrees clockwise, assuming a riding stance by stamping down with the left foot as you execute a W block with both forearms.

FINAL FRONT VIEW

TOP VIEW

APPLICATION

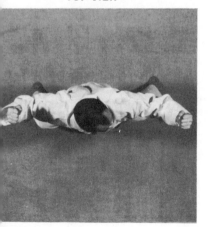

BEGINNING FRONT VIEW

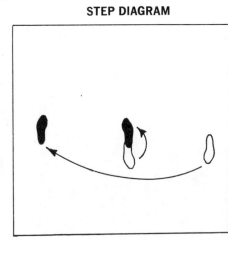

INTERMEDIATE FRONT VIEW

OTHER VIEW

STEP DIAGRAM

15. SAN MARKI
(Stamping W Block)

Pivot on the right foot 180 degrees clockwise, assuming a riding stance by stamping down with the left foot as you execute a W block with both forearms.

FINAL FRONT VIEW

TOP VIEW

APPLICATION

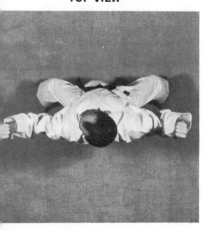

BEGINNING FRONT VIEW

INTERMEDIATE FRONT VIEW

OTHER VIEW

STEP DIAGRAM

16. SAN MARKI

(Stamping W Block)

Pivot on the left foot 180 degrees counterclockwise, assuming a riding stance by stamping down with the right foot as you execute a W block with both forearms.

FINAL FRONT VIEW

TOP VIEW

APPLICATION

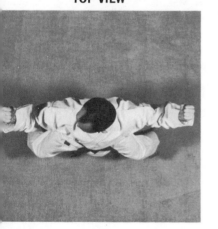

BEGINNING FRONT VIEW

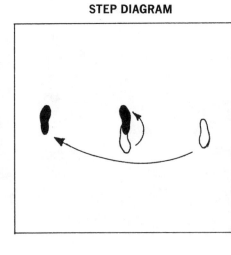

INTERMEDIATE FRONT VIEW

OTHER VIEW

STEP DIAGRAM

17. SAN MARKI
(Stamping W Block)

Pivot on the right foot 180 degrees clockwise, assuming a riding stance by stamping down with the left foot as you execute a W block with both forearms.

FINAL FRONT VIEW

TOP VIEW

APPLICATION

BEGINNING FRONT VIEW

INTERMEDIATE FRONT VIEW

OTHER VIEW

STEP DIAGRAM

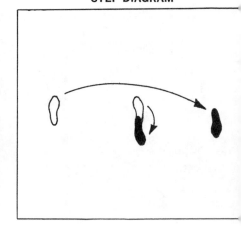

FINAL FRONT VIEW

18. SAN MARKI
(Stamping W Block)

Pivot on the right foot 180 degrees clockwise, assuming a riding stance by stamping down with the left foot as you execute a W block with both forearms.

TOP VIEW

APPLICATION

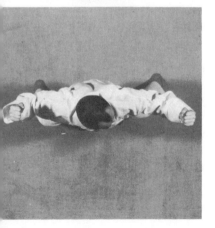

BEGINNING FRONT VIEW

INTERMEDIATE FRONT VIEW

OTHER VIEW

STEP DIAGRAM

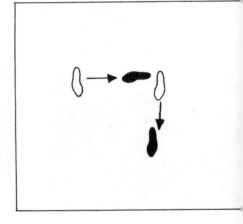

128

19. HARDAN DO PALMOK MARKI
(Low Double Forearm Block)

Bring the right foot alongside the left foot, then take a straight step with the left foot, assuming a right back stance as you execute a low block with double forearms.

FINAL FRONT VIEW

TOP VIEW

APPLICATION

BEGINNING FRONT VIEW

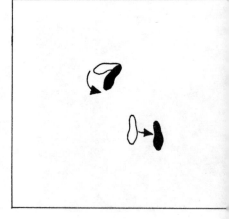

INTERMEDIATE FRONT VIEW

OTHER VIEW

STEP DIAGRAM

130

FINAL FRONT VIEW

20. MORI JARPKI
(Head Grabbing)

Slide the left foot forward, assuming a left front stance as you extend both hands upward in a grabbing motion.

TOP VIEW	APPLICATION

BEGINNING FRONT VIEW

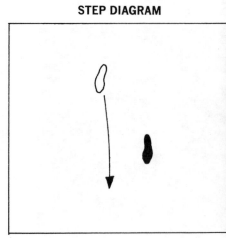

INTERMEDIATE FRONT VIEW

OTHER VIEW

STEP DIAGRAM

21. MURUP CHAGI
(Knee Kick)

Pull both hands downward as you execute a middle kick with the right knee. ✦

FINAL FRONT VIEW

TOP VIEW

APPLICATION

BEGINNING FRONT VIEW

INTERMEDIATE FRONT VIEW

OTHER VIEW

STEP DIAGRAM

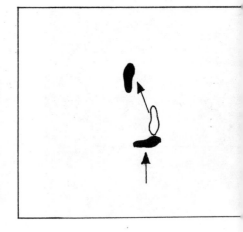

134

FINAL FRONT VIEW

22. CHUNGDAN SUDO

(Middle Knife-Hand Block)

Lower the right foot alongside the left foot, then pivot on the right foot 180 degrees counterclockwise, assuming a right back stance as you execute a middle knife-hand block with the left knife-hand.

TOP VIEW

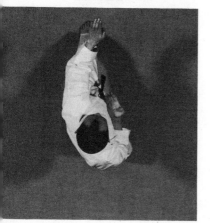

APPLICATION

OTHER VIEW

STEP DIAGRAM

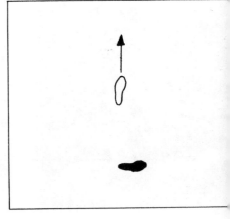

FINAL FRONT VIEW

23. HARDAN AP CHAGI
(Low Front Snap Kick)

Execute a low front snap kick with the left foot without changing hand positions.

TOP VIEW

APPLICATION

BEGINNING FRONT VIEW

INTERMEDIATE FRONT VIEW

OTHER VIEW

STEP DIAGRAM

24. SANGDAN KWANSU

(High Spear-Finger)

Take a straight step with the kicking foot, assuming a left front stance as you execute a high spear-finger thrust with the left hand.

FINAL FRONT VIEW

TOP VIEW

APPLICATION

BEGINNING FRONT VIEW

INTERMEDIATE FRONT VIEW

OTHER VIEW

STEP DIAGRAM

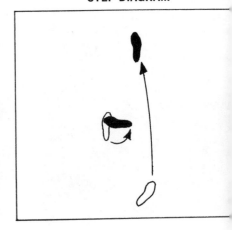

25.CHUNGDAN SUDO MARKI

(Middle Knife-Hand Block)

Take a straight step with the right foot, assuming a left back stance as you execute a middle knife-hand block with the right knife-hand.

FINAL FRONT VIEW

TOP VIEW

APPLICATION

BEGINNING FRONT VIEW

INTERMEDIATE FRONT VIEW

OTHER VIEW

STEP DIAGRAM

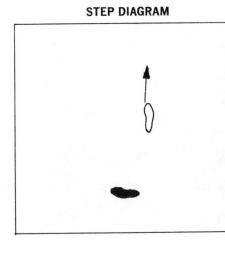

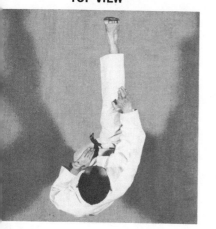

FINAL FRONT VIEW

26. HARDAN AP CHAGI

(Low Front Snap Kick)

Execute a low front snap kick with the right foot without changing hand positions.

TOP VIEW

APPLICATION

BEGINNING FRONT VIEW

INTERMEDIATE FRONT VIEW

OTHER VIEW

STEP DIAGRAM

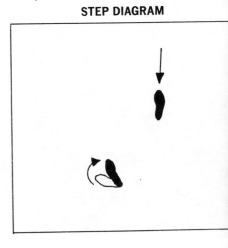

FINAL FRONT VIEW

27. SANGDAN KWANSU
(High Spear-Finger)

Take a straight step with the kicking foot, assuming a right front stance as you execute a high spear-finger thrust with the right hand.

TOP VIEW

APPLICATION

145

BEGINNING FRONT VIEW

INTERMEDIATE FRONT VIEW

OTHER VIEW

STEP DIAGRAM

28. SANGDAN YIKWON TAERIGI HARDAN PALMOK MARKI

(High Back Fist Strike and Low Forearm Block)

Pull the right foot back, assuming a right back stance as you execute a high strike with the right back fist and a low block with the left forearm.

FINAL FRONT VIEW

TOP VIEW

APPLICATION

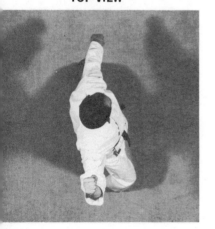

BEGINNING FRONT VIEW

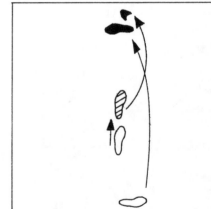

INTERMEDIATE FRONT VIEW

OTHER VIEW

STEP DIAGRAM

FINAL FRONT VIEW

29.HARDAN KYOCHA SOGI KYOCHA JOOMOK MARKI

(Low X Stance X Fist Block After Jump)

Jump forward, landing in a right X stance as you execute a low X fist block.

TOP VIEW

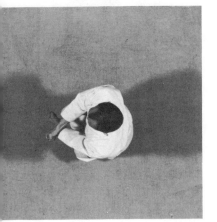

APPLICATION

BEGINNING FRONT VIEW   **INTERMEDIATE FRONT VIEW**

OTHER VIEW   **STEP DIAGRAM**

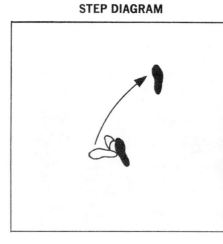

30. SANGDAN DO PALMOK MARKI

(High Double Forearm Block)

Pivot on the left foot 90 degrees clockwise, assuming a right front stance as you execute a high block with the right double forearm.

FINAL FRONT VIEW

TOP VIEW

APPLICATION

BEGINNING FRONT VIEW

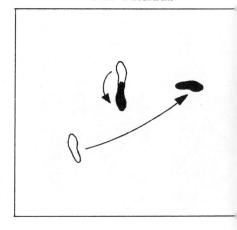

INTERMEDIATE FRONT VIEW

OTHER VIEW

STEP DIAGRAM

152

31. HARDAN SUDO MARKI

(Low Knife-Hand Block)

Pivot on the right foot 270 degrees counterclockwise, assuming a right back stance as you execute a low block with the left knife-hand.

FINAL FRONT VIEW

TOP VIEW

APPLICATION

BEGINNING FRONT VIEW

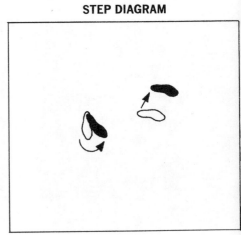

INTERMEDIATE FRONT VIEW

OTHER VIEW

STEP DIAGRAM

32. TOLYO MARKI
(Circular Block)

Slide the left foot forward, assuming a left front stance as you execute a circular block with the right inner forearm.

FINAL FRONT VIEW

TOP VIEW

APPLICATION

BEGINNING FRONT VIEW

INTERMEDIATE FRONT VIEW

OTHER VIEW

STEP DIAGRAM

FINAL FRONT VIEW

33. HARDAN SUDO MARKI
(Low Knife-Hand Block)

Bring the left foot alongside the right foot, then step out with the right foot, assuming a left back stance as you execute a low block with the right knife-hand.

TOP VIEW

APPLICATION

BEGINNING FRONT VIEW

INTERMEDIATE FRONT VIEW

OTHER VIEW

STEP DIAGRAM

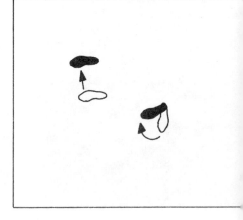

34. TOLYO MARKI
(Circular Block)

Slide the right foot forward, assuming a right front stance as you execute a circular block with the left inner forearm.

FINAL FRONT VIEW

TOP VIEW

APPLICATION

BEGINNING FRONT VIEW

INTERMEDIATE FRONT VIEW

OTHER VIEW

STEP DIAGRAM

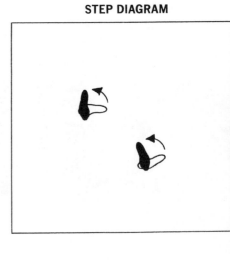

FINAL FRONT VIEW

35. TOLYO MARKI
(Circular Block)

Assume a left front stance as you execute a circular block with the right inner forearm.

TOP VIEW

APPLICATION

BEGINNING FRONT VIEW

INTERMEDIATE FRONT VIEW

OTHER VIEW

STEP DIAGRAM

36. TOLYO MARKI
(Circular Block)

Assume a right front stance as you execute a circular block with the left inner forearm.

FINAL FRONT VIEW

TOP VIEW

APPLICATION

BEGINNING FRONT VIEW

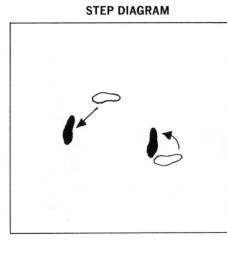

INTERMEDIATE FRONT VIEW

OTHER VIEW

STEP DIAGRAM

FINAL FRONT VIEW

37. KIMA SOGI CHIRUGI
(Middle Riding Stance Punch)

Slide the right foot forward, assuming a riding stance as you execute a middle punch with the right fist.✱

TOP VIEW

APPLICATION

SIDE VIEW

BACK VIEW

OTHER VIEW

STEP DIAGRAM

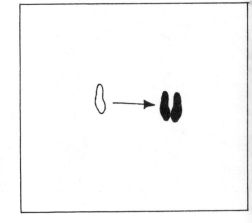

FRONT VIEW

GOMAN
(End)

Bring the left foot alongside the right foot, assuming a closed ready stance "B" with left open hand covering right fist at solar-plexus level.

TOP VIEW

APPLICATION